D1302301

MUELLER'S OFFICIAL PUPPY OWNER'S MANUAL

Is Published By
Bridgeport Publishing
P.O. Box 215
Blacklick, Ohio 43004

Written By
Scott Mueller, Director
National K-9 School Of Dog Trainers

Illustrations By
Drew Robinson

Edited By
Amelie G. Bush

Library Of Congress Catalog Card Number 93-90501

ISBN 0-9637183-0-4

Important Data

Puppy's Name _____

Breed _____ Sex _____

Dates: Birth _____ Purchased _____

Markings _____

License#_____Tattoo#_____

AKC#_____

Owner:
　　Name _____

　　Address _____

　　City _____ State __ ZIP_____

　　Telephone (Home) _____

　　Telephone (Work) _____

Veterinarian:
　　Name ._____

　　Address _____

　　Telephone _____

Breeder/Seller:
　　Name _____

　　Address _____

　　Telephone _____

Puppy Health Record

Age	Date	Distemper	Hepatitis	Leptospirosis	Parainfluenza	Bordetella	Parvovirus	Corona	Rabies	
____ Weeks	____	☐	☐	☐	☐	☐	☐	☐	☐	☐
____ Weeks	____	☐	☐	☐	☐	☐	☐	☐	☐	☐
____ Weeks	____	☐	☐	☐	☐	☐	☐	☐	☐	☐
____ Months	____	☐	☐	☐	☐	☐	☐	☐	☐	☐
____ Months	____	☐	☐	☐	☐	☐	☐	☐	☐	☐
1 Year	____	☐	☐	☐	☐	☐	☐	☐	☐	☐
2 Year	____	☐	☐	☐	☐	☐	☐	☐	☐	☐

Heartworm Test

Age	Date	Pos	Neg	Comments
_____	_____	☐	☐	_____
_____	_____	☐	☐	_____
_____	_____	☐	☐	_____

Fecal Exam

Age	Date	Pos	Neg	Comments
_____	_____	☐	☐	_____
_____	_____	☐	☐	_____
_____	_____	☐	☐	_____

Table Of Contents

DEDICATION

This book is dedicated to the most important dog in the world, your new puppy. The author of this booklet sincerely hopes that the materials contained within will provide you with the information necessary for a lifetime of joy and happiness with your new canine friend.

FOREWORD

There are few joys like owning a puppy. But, with this joy comes responsibility — responsibility to your dog, yourself, your family and your neighborhood. Puppies are blissfully ignorant about what is required of them. You must learn how to approach and guide your puppy so that he will develop into a good canine citizen, one with whom you will want to share your home.

Inside this booklet you will find all of the information you need to help you develop a successful long-term relationship with your puppy. Read it thoroughly, as it was written to help all new puppy owners better understand and care for their new pet through proper socialization and training.

The age old saying, "An ounce of prevention is worth a pound of cure," has never been more appropriate than when it comes to raising a puppy. Yet many puppy owners develop a "wait and see" attitude instead of taking an active role in guiding their puppy's development. All puppies count on their owners for guidance. And your puppy is counting on you.

1

TOPIC 1-KEEPING YOUR PUPPY HEALTHY

Before You Bring Your New Puppy Home

Before you purchase or accept a new puppy, there are certai health-related points you should check. His eyes should b clear and bright with no excessive mucous discharge. His nos should be clean with no purulent nasal discharge, and his ear should look clean and free of excessive wax. Look at his coat. I it clean without excessive dryness or flakiness and is it free o fleas or other external parasites? A potbellied appearance or dis tended abdomen may be an indication of intestinal parasites o worms. Both the puppy and his environment should be clean.

Nursing puppies will acquire some immunity from their moth ers. The maternal antibodies in the colostrum or initial milk wil

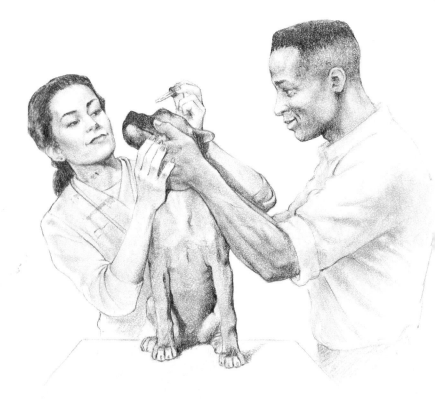

ive puppies a passive immunity against the diseases that the mother has been exposed to or vaccinated against. Since the maternal protection gradually decreases, it is hard to predict when it loses its effectiveness. Therefore, if at all possible, have your puppy examined by a veterinarian within 24 hours of bringing him home. If not, have him checked as soon as possible during his first week in his new home.

Vaccines

It is suggested puppies receive their first vaccinations at six to eight weeks of age, and continued vaccinations at three to four week intervals until the puppy is sixteen to eighteen weeks old. The following vaccines are necessary to prevent life threatening illnesses. Most veterinarians use combination vaccines (*) that offer protection against several diseases with one injection.

*Distemper
*Hepatitis
*Leptospirosis
*Parainfluenza
*Parvovirus
Rabies — Given separately

Two other vaccines, Corona and Bordetella, are offered for puppies who frequent parks and kennels where the chances of exposure to other diseases is greatly increased. You will want to seek the advice of your veterinarian as to the necessity of these for your puppy.

Required Health Tests
Intestinal Parasites (worms) — Hooks, Whips, Tapes and Round Worms
Your puppy should be tested for internal parasites as soon as possible. These worms live in the intestines, literally sucking the blood and nutrients from his intestinal walls. They can also cause vomiting, restlessness and bloody diarrhea. An infestation of worms can severely weaken your puppy and make him a target for other forms of bacterial or viral diseases.

Take a small stool sample (fecal sample) and have it examined at your veterinarian's office at least once every three to four months until your puppy is one year old. This is an inexpensive test and is imperative for your puppy's health as he develops into an adult dog.

Heartworms

This deadly disease became a serious concern not too many years ago in the southern portion of the United States and spread rapidly into the rest of the country by the mid 80's. Infection in the dog begins when larvae from an infective mosquito are injected under the skin The larvae migrate through the dog's tissues into a vein move to the heart and become sexually mature. Adult worms usually make their home in the right atrium, the right ventricle, and the arteries of the lungs. Worms in the lungs block the flow of blood out of the right side of the heart. Worms entwined about the heart valves interfere with the mechanics of the heart. According to medical sources, as many as 250 adult worms have been found in a dog.

The only way to test for the disease is through a blood test You will want to put your dog on a preventive program during the mosquito season. This will vary depending on geographical region. Consult your veterinarian for his/her recommendation Today some veterinarians recommend year round protection.

Heat Stress/Stroke

Precautions must be taken to insure that your puppy is not kept in a hot unventilated area. A common mistake made by many owners is leaving a dog unsupervised in an area without shade, ventilation and/or water. Heat can build up quickly in these areas, causing heat stress. Heat stress can cause a dog's body temperature to rise to the dangerous level of 106 degrees or higher. These high temperatures often lead to convulsions that can cause permanent brain damage. In extreme cases, heat stress can cause heart failure and death.

Puppies and Poisons

Puppies, like small children, must be protected from poisons. Many household plants and products contain substances that are toxic to your puppy. Because puppies are so curious, it is important to keep these items out of reach or behind closed/locked doors. If you suspect exposure, call your veterinarian with the

4

ame and quantity of items ingested. Keep your veterinarian's mergency number near the phone. Listed below are typical ousehold items that can cause severe reactions or even death if wallowed:

Antifreeze (ethylene glycol) - watch driveways and parking lots, ogs love the sweet taste.

Rat and mice poisons (anticoagulant chemicals)

Chocolate (theobromine)

Household cleaners and detergents

Seasonal plants such as mistletoe, poinsettia and holly berries

Houseplants such as dieffenbachia and philodendron

Spaying and Neutering

Unless you are a serious breeder, both you and your dog will be happier if you neuter or spay your animal. Raising a litter of puppies may seem like a lot of fun, but in reality, it is a lot of work and can be quite expensive. Most females go into heat twice a year, with approximately 14 to 21 days of potential bloody discharge that can play havoc with your carpets. Of course, there is the real possibility of an accidental pregnancy. Additionally, you may be left with a number of puppies that you are unable to sell or place into good homes.

Neutering a male dog can help prevent prostate gland problems such as cancer, while spaying a female will not only eliminate the possibility of ovarian cancer but will also significantly reduce the risk of mammary gland tumors or cancer.

If, however, after successfully raising your dog you are still determined to become a breeder, have your dog evaluated by professional canine judges and research current breeding and market trends. The library and your local breed club are good places to begin.

TOPIC 2-THE DOMESTICATION AND SOCIALIZATION OF YOUR PUPPY

Sooner Is Better Than Later: The familiar phrase "A dog is man's best friend" may come under question by owners who purchase puppies assuming that if they simply feed and love their puppy, they will have the perfect pet. While puppies certainly are intelligent animals, they have to be molded to their environment and taught proper etiquette, such as using the bathroom outside or not chewing on the furniture. It is easier to prevent unwanted behavior than to correct or break a bad habit later, if at all.

Bringing Your New Puppy Home: Coming home is a time of adventure and excitement for your new puppy. Because puppies are irresistibly cuddly and cute, everyone wants to give them lots of attention. While these social contacts are good for your puppy's domestic growth, too much of a fuss will quickly spoil him and he will expect this kind of attention when it is not appropriate. Ask your friends and family members to refrain from doing more than a simple pat on the head unless your puppy seems afraid of or nervous around strangers. Then more social contact is appropriate to help him overcome his fears.

Establishing a few simple rules (for your puppy and your family) right from the beginning will reap many rewards later. For example, during the first two to six months of your puppy's life it will be important to set up daytime play and sleeping areas where you can keep an eye on him. Housebreaking and other behavior modifications will be much easier if you are near him or have some control over his space. Although puppy crates and pens are sometimes thought of as cruel by people who have not used them, they actually offer comfort and security for both you and your new pet and can be used very effectively while dealing with early puppy training.

Nighttime is usually one of the more difficult times to enforce "area rules" as most new puppy owners are tempted to allow their new pet to sleep on furniture or in bed with them. Your puppy will be missing his litter mates and will appear to be lonely. You will feel sorry for him and will be tempted to cuddle with him and even take him to bed with you. If you give into his cries he will quickly learn that he can easily have his way with you and will continue to cry for attention. Be prepared to use your will power. Remember, puppies spoil as easily as children. It is best to keep his sleeping area in a convenient place close to you, yet convenient to the out of doors for bathroom runs. This is usually a good time to use a puppy crate.

Correcting your puppy; It is seldom necessary to discipline a puppy. Generally most forms of correction can be given with a semi firm shaking of the scruff of his neck and a stern "no". You must never lose your temper when correcting your puppy, nor should you hold a grudge against him. Do not discipline him by putting him in his cage, throwing him out of doors or sending him to the basement. Your puppy is not capable of understanding this kind of correction. Most acts of transgression for which your puppy needs to be corrected are simple misunderstandings of what is right and wrong and not acts of stubbornness or spitefulness.

How Puppies Learn: Puppies are often said to be creatures of habit who learn by association. By age six weeks most puppies are capable of the full use of their senses such as sight, hearing and smell. It is at this time that a puppy begins recording messages, both good and bad, much like a tape recorder (see illustration on following page) or a computer bank. Later, when an unknown sight, sound or smell is sensed or an unfamiliar person comes near them, they will refer to this stored knowledge to form a positive or negative response. For example, if a puppy has been favorably introduced to the postal carrier, when he grows up he will not fear or growl at him or her every time the mail is delivered.

The most critical learning or association period usually takes place during the first sixteen weeks of the puppy's life (most often from six weeks to sixteen weeks). During this time it is important to begin to teach your puppy right from wrong. Waiting until a puppy is six months to a year old to begin training is a mistake and risks allowing his behavior to get out of hand. Remember, a puppy's attitude toward life and his environment is generally formed by the time he is sixteen weeks of age.

Remember too that puppies, like children, learn in individual patterns and at different rates. Some will learn to sit or will housebreak with little effort while others may require more of your patience. Continue reading this booklet. In the next section we will talk about introducing your puppy to the people, animals and objects in his new environment.

The All Important Puppy Pre-School: One of the most critical types of training for your new puppy begins the moment

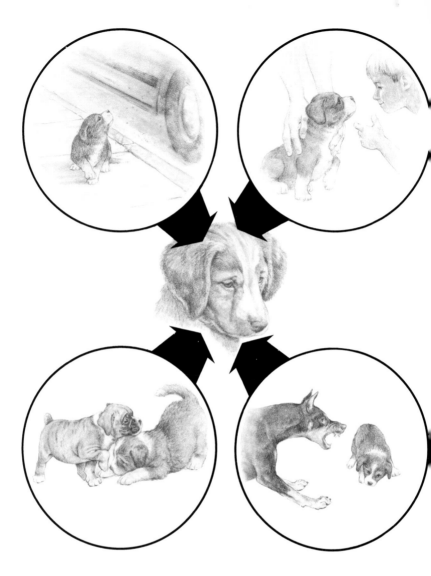

you bring him home. Early socialization training (Puppy Pre-School) is the heart of domesticating your puppy to live with you in your environment and is the foundation for successful obedience training and a lifetime of communication.

Through socialization, your puppy will learn to trust. This training must be carried out during the entire first 16 weeks of the puppy's life. Puppies who are not socialized at an early age develop fears which tend to regress into patterns of behavior much like those of their undomesticated relatives, causing many problems or today's dog owners. For example, dogs who are not socialized (introduced) to children as young pups will often grow up to fear them. This fear may lead to undesirable aggressive behavior towards children as the pup grows older. All too often the dog is not mean or unnecessarily aggressive but is simply reacting to an unfamiliar situation in the only way he knows how. Sadly, once a dog bites or attacks a child, there is usually little hope that socialization will make any difference and usually the dog has to be euthanized.

The key to proper socialization is controlling the environment in which the puppy learns so that he retains the same value/behavioral system exhibited by his owner. This does not mean protecting him from the world; it simply means supervising the process so that he will ultimately have positive recorded messages from which to draw later in life. This is also a good time to purchase a training collar and leash. For his own safety, the dog will need some leash control during socialization. It is also wise to prepare your puppy for trips in the car since you will probably need to travel away from home to introduce him to some of the people and elements of society.

Begin taking your puppy in the car with someone holding him on their lap. Bring along a small toy or treat. You may want to purchase a car carry case or a puppy seat belt. Start with short jaunts (around the block) and gradually build to one hour road trips. A good way to prevent initial car/motion sickness is to keep your puppy from seeing out the window. Once he is accustomed to taking rides in the car, this will normally go away and you will not need to restrict his vision. It is also important to wait at least one hour after eating before taking him for a ride.

All puppies should go for rides in the car other than to the veterinarian. These rides are a good time to stop at parks or playgrounds and introduce your puppy to children.

Introducing Your Puppy To People: Human socialization is the most important part of domestication and should begin the moment you bring your new puppy home if he is to learn to trust the people with whom he will be living. Undoubtedly the most important form of domestication is socializing him around people of all sizes, shapes, races and ages. Many people make the mistake of thinking that if they introduce their puppy to the neighbors he will become more loyal to them and go to them or spend more time in their yard. This is simply not true, but a dog who has not been properly socialized to a variety of people may eventually bite or attack when exposed to them later in life.

Each week make two or three trips around the neighborhood and town. Select stops that will offer a variety of experiences such as parks, shopping centers and playgrounds. A wide range of friendly people performing different tasks will provide your puppy with positive memories and give him no reasons to fear. Be sure to include children, particularly small children and crawling infants. Puppies have been known to attack babies by unintentionally misinterpreting their crawling body language for another animal. Supervising your puppy is the key to avoiding accidental harm.

If You Are Expecting A Baby: We have all heard horror stories about dogs attacking young children and babies. Based on years of experience, I believe that most of these horrible situations could have been avoided with proper socialization and training.

If you are expecting a baby, I would suggest purchasing a baby doll (approximately life size) from your local toy store several weeks before the baby is due. Begin the ritual of taking the baby doll out of the crib or bassinet in front of your dog at least once a day. Place the doll on the floor where your dog can observe you diapering and powdering it. As you are doing this, reach over and give your dog a reassuring and calm pat on the head as though he were sharing in the excitement. Pay close attention to the reaction of your dog as you fuss over the doll. Do not forget to talk to your dog in a soft and friendly manner. If you want to carry this exercise a bit further, purchase a doll that cries, or use a sound effects CD or tape.

If your dog appears to be too upset or growls at the doll, take these threats seriously. Consult a professional dog trainer for further advice. Never take any chances with babies and puppies. Your puppy may not normally show aggression but may feel threatened by another small being that appears to be taking up his space and time. Puppies do not know a baby is a baby unless they are taught through early socialization and training.

Introducing Your Puppy To Other Animals: The frequency with which you introduce your puppy to other animal groups may depend upon where you live. But, if you make an effort to always introduce him to animals of good nature, he will record only positive messages and will be less likely to grow up to be an animal fighter, terrorizing the neighborhood.

Socialize your puppy around other well-behaved dogs and puppies several times a week for the first four months of his life. This should create a permanent positive message that will last the rest of his life and will likely counter his innate feelings when he does come across a non-social dog.

Introducing Your Puppy To Household Appliances and Yard Equipment: A small amount of fear, or what might be termed "healthy respect," is sometimes a good thing when it comes to mechanical objects. The purpose of socialization training is to prevent unreasonable fears.

Allow your puppy to investigate some objects on his own. For example, if you are attempting to introduce your puppy to the vacuum cleaner, do not immediately turn it on and run it toward him. Instead, run it around him while it is turned off. This same approach can be used with other electrical appliances, such as hairdryers. I also recommend playing ball around a potentially fearful object, allowing the ball to bounce and roll on and off of it. As your puppy plays with the ball he will begin to realize that neither he nor the ball are being hurt by the piece of equipment.

Do not allow your friends or family members to tease your puppy with mechanical objects during this important period in his life. He will not think it is fun and he will develop an unreasonable fear of the object. For example (although this is not a mechanical device), do not allow people to shake and spray cans of pop around the puppy. They may think his fearful reaction to the fizzing and spraying is funny but the sound alone may very well cause him to be afraid of water, thunderstorms and other similar sounds for the rest of his life. This could include giving him a bath.

Depending upon where you live, here is a short list of typical objects to which puppies should be introduced during their early socialization training:

automobiles	baby strollers
barbecue grills	farm machinery
garbage trucks	hairdryers
ironing board	motorcycles
metal garbage cans with lids	bicycles
power brooms	power mowers
snow blowers	trucks
umbrellas	vacuum sweepers

Note: This is only a sample list of household appliances. Checl
your own home and yard and then make a list of all of the thing
to which you want to introduce your puppy.

TOPIC 3-FEEDING AND HOUSEBREAKING

Your Puppy's Food

Avoid the temptation of giving your puppy scraps from you
plate. This will begin the habit of begging as well as grab
bing food out of unsuspecting (such as children's) hands. Feeding
should be done on a fixed schedule using a food that is designec
for a growing puppy. Because much research has gone into the
development of today's dog food products, it may not be importan
which major brand name food you choose. However, there are
some puppies who cannot handle cereal-based products yet dc
very well with meat by-products, or the other way around.

If your puppy develops a persistent loose stool, take him tc
your veterinarian for a check-up. It could be as simple as an aller
gy to food supplements or food types. Most puppies who suffei
from these allergies are placed on a lamb and rice diet. (Intestina
parasites can also be the cause of a loose stool).

Vitamin supplements are not usually necessary for today's
puppy, simply because most foods are fortified with additional vit
amins and minerals. Offering extra vitamins to a puppy who does
not need them can create a health problem. However, if you have
a large-boned puppy who gets lots of exercise and does not ea
well, your veterinarian may want to offer him some additional vit
amins. In any case, consult your puppy's doctor.

Puppies between the ages of 7 and 12 weeks should be fec
three times a day regardless of breed, but preferably no more thar
four times per day, with the exception of large breeds expected tc

grow in excess of 100 pounds. Leaving food down throughout the day presents a problem because your puppy will pick at it all day, causing irregular bowel habits and making housebreaking nearly impossible.

If you find your puppy consistently does not eat one of the scheduled meals, eliminate it altogether. Your puppy will eat only what his system requires. You will have to trust him. Just like people, puppies will require different amounts of food. In fact, many puppies are picky eaters and generally look rather lean until they reach 2 to 3 years of age.

Snacks: Giving your puppy a small snack as a reward for indicating his need followed by going outside is fine, but be sure these snacks do not interfere with his eating habits. Frequently these snacks are so good that your puppy might not eat his regular food, holding out for a later treat.

The best snacks are plain hard small milkbones, or their equivalents, as they are good for teething and rarely spoil appetites. These are not only healthy, but are also a great way to help keep your dog's teeth clean.

Crate Training: Without a doubt the easiest and best way to prevent misbehavior such as inappropriate chewing or house-

breaking accidents is the use of a crate, known as a puppy cage a.k.a. pen. Feeding your puppy in his pen will give him a positive association with it. Using the crate allows you to leave your home or work uninterrupted for anywhere from a few minutes to a few hours. These "playpens" will prevent your puppy from hurting himself or getting into trouble. Additionally, if your puppy is safely tucked away in his cage, it is praise not correction that he will hear from you first when you return home. Never use the crate for discipline. It should be used just as you would use a child's playpen.

Never leave your puppy in his crate while he is wearing a collar (especially a training collar). All it takes is a few minutes for him to accidentally choke himself. Also, always be sure to remove any potentially harmful objects from his pen.

Note: Crate illustrated shows a section of wall cut to fit, allowing you to adjust his amount of freedom during the housebreaking period and preventing him from wandering to the back of the cage for a bathroom area. Once he is housebroken, this section can be removed.

Housebreaking Your Puppy: Your puppy will not housebreak himself. Housebreaking takes a concerted effort of understanding and consistent direction on your part. It is through consistent conditioning and repetitive exercises for several weeks that your puppy becomes familiar with his routine. It may take up to six months before he can be 100 percent housebroken. Don't assume your puppy is housebroken before that time. Remember too, your puppy looks to you for guidance and it is up to you to provide it. The following information is intended to provide guidelines for housebreaking that have been developed during my 20 years as a trainer.

Be sure your puppy is free of intestinal parasites. Parasites (worms) cause puppies to have loose and irregular bowel movements, making housebreaking difficult to impossible.

It is a natural instinct for puppies to seek an area away from their den to relieve themselves. Therefore it is wise to begin by restricting your puppy's freedom in the house through the use of a pen or escape-proof crate. Without a cage or 24-hour-a-day direct supervision, your puppy will choose his den as well as his bathroom areas. Your guidance is critical for your puppy's development.

At night, just before you go to bed, secure your puppy in his crate. Do not give in to him if he cries or whines. Puppies are creatures of habit and if he learns that his fussing causes you to give in to his desires, you could be in for many sleepless nights. Do, however, give him one last opportunity to go outside before you go to bed.

In order to teach your puppy where he is to use the bathroom, you must take him to the same area every time. You must also stay with him, praising him verbally as he relieves himself. This step is essential in helping your puppy understand it is OK to use the bathroom in your presence as long as he does it where he is supposed to. Your puppy will also learn to associate a specific command such as, "hurry up" or "do your business" with this exercise. Soon he will understand the purpose and will look forward to his visits.

Many people today continue to use the old method of laying newspaper down on the kitchen floor and encouraging their puppy to go on the newspaper. The problem with this method is that it makes it harder for them to ever learn to go outside. Also, many dogs tend to stand on the paper with their front feet and miss with their back ones. Newspaper training is messy and smelly at best.

If you purchased your puppy from a pet store or breeder who used newspaper, you will need to take several pieces of paper outside to the areas you wish your puppy to use. Use some stones to hold the papers down. Then, take your puppy to that spot each time you want him to go. If you have a small dog, pick a place close to the house (especially in cold weather and snow). After several days remove the newspapers altogether.

Note: Newspapers can be used by people who must leave their puppies at home alone while they are at work and have no one to let the puppy out to relieve himself. Use a large pen (crate), putting his bedding in the front half and newspaper in the back half. As he becomes old enough (6-7 months), you can begin removing the newspaper on the days when you are at home. Replace the newspaper with bedding materials. If the papers are not there he will hold his bathroom needs much longer. At these times you can begin to teach your dog to wait several hours between bathroom trips, building up to 5 to 8 hours by the time he is 7 to 8 months old.

Any time your pup defecates or urinates outside, he deserves some free time in the house to play ball or just wander around being with you. This will help your puppy appreciate his responsibility to relieve himself out of doors. This time should also be supervised so that he does not get into mischief. No puppy will immediately succeed at housebreaking. All puppies will have accidents now and then, but you must catch them in the act to correct them. As each day goes by, allow your pup a little more freedom between bathroom exercises to see if he runs to the door when he needs to go. Don't be surprised, however, if he chooses to wander off into the dining room and squat behind the table. Instead, be ready for it and reprimand him as he begins to squat. This reprimand should consist of no more than a mild shaking and a stern "no," followed by taking him outdoors.

Time Schedule: By regulating the feeding schedule of your puppy you will quickly discover that he will have a need to relieve himself at approximately the same times each day. For example, for an 8 week old puppy, if your last feeding is 5:00 PM, your puppy will usually need to go outside within fifteen minutes and will have his last bowel movement for the night sometime between 8 and 11 PM. As you proceed with housebreaking, stretch the day's bathroom trips further apart each week, by 15 minute intervals, so that your puppy has to control his bathroom necessities. Soon you will be able to sleep in on some occasions, especially as your puppy becomes older. Because of various sizes of breeds, some puppies will have to go out more often than others. The following chart is simply a sample to help illustrate the correlation between food and water and bathroom exercises. Obviously you will have to make your own chart, one that fits your life and daily schedule. (X denotes your time to feed, water or exercise your puppy)

(See chart on next page)

16

Sample Time Schedule For An 8 To 12 Week Old Puppy

Duplicate This Chart And Use On A Daily Basis

DATE: _____   INITIALS: _____

Time	Feed	Water	Bathroom Exercise
6:30am			X
6:45am	X	X	
7:00am			X
Noon			X
12:15pm	*(Optional)	X	
12:30pm			X
3:30pm		X	X
5:00pm	X	X	
5:15pm			X
8:00pm		X	X
11:00pm			X
11:05pm	Bedtime (Crate)		

*Some dogs will need this additional feeding.

Housebreaking discipline: Catching your puppy in the act of doing something that you do not approve of will require immediate attention in the form of discipline, but only if you catch him in the act. Any discipline after the fact will only confuse your puppy and cause him to unjustly fear you. Corrections should be swift and to the point, consisting of a soft spank on the bottom or shake of the scruff on his neck saying "no" or "no bad puppy" followed by taking him out to the bathroom area to complete or finish what he attempted to do in the house. This is then followed by praise.

The most common mistake made by puppy owners is correcting a puppy after the fact. Example: you come home from work and find your puppy has defecated on the floor in the house. You discipline him by rubbing his nose in it or yelling at him. That may make you feel better, but, because your pup is not capable of understanding or associating the correction with the crime, it will have little or even a negative impact on him. The only way corrections will work is if you catch your puppy in the act or appearing to be looking for a place to go. Then, tell him no and run him outside to the area where he is supposed to go and praise him as he goes in front of you at the designated bathroom area.

Summary Of Basic Rules For Housebreaking:
1. Be sure your puppy is free of worms and other parasites.
2. Use the cage or crate when you cannot directly supervise your puppy.
3. Stay outside with your puppy so that you can praise him while he is learning his bathroom habits.
4. Give your puppy ample time to do his business but also teach him the words "hurry up," snapping his leash if he wastes time sniffing too long or playing. Save the play time for afterward.
5. After a successful bathroom exercise, play with your puppy, or allow him to wander around the house with you.
6. Follow the time schedule faithfully (feed, water, and bathroom visits), using the same times daily.
-Do not overfeed your puppy or give him more meals per day than recommended (cut out a feeding if your puppy is having great difficulty in housebreaking).
-Do not feed your puppy table scraps or between meal snacks (except those discussed in this section)
-Do not give your pup water within an hour of bedtime unless heat conditions warrant it
-Do not leave his food out for longer than fifteen minutes
7. Do not reprimand him for an accident unless you catch him in the act.
8. Be patient. The effort put in now will last your dog's lifetime.
9. Be consistent.

Cleaning Accidents: All accidents should be cleaned as quickly as possible using a mild solution of ammonia, water and vinegar. This masks the odor and prevents your puppy from smelling the soiled area and repeating his action. Other cleaning products are available at your local pet store.

TOPIC 4-DEALING WITH ANNOYING HABITS

Breaking The Chewing Habit: Puppies chew for a variety of reasons. Most of these reasons are perfectly normal, the main one being teething. Puppies begin teething as young as four weeks and generally have a strong need to chew until their teeth have all come in, around six months of age.

During this period of time it is important to supply your puppy with proper chew toys — ones that will alleviate his desire to chew without turning him into a permanent chewer. This is usually a good time to provide him with a toy box that is his and has only his chew toys in it.

Just as our children need safe teething rings so, too, do our puppies need safe toys to aid in their teething discomfort. Correcting your puppy for chewing during teething will only confuse him since he really cannot help himself. Instead, supply him with a safe chew toy such as a heavy sock scented with peppermint extract so that he knows the difference.

Some puppies chew out of boredom. Puppies who are left alone for long periods of time without some kind of constructive activity often turn to chewing. To prevent this, make every effort to teach your puppy what he can and can't chew on in your home. This is a good time to use your puppy crate/pen. If you are unable to supervise your puppy, put him in his crate with his chew toys. I also recommend leaving a radio or television on for your puppy if you are going to be away for any long period of time. This will alleviate some of the loneliness during solitary confinement.

Poor diet can be another reason your puppy is chewing. If your puppy is not getting enough chewing action from his food he may turn to other items such as your furniture. Sometimes a change in food, to one that requires more chewing, will solve this problem.

If you catch your puppy chewing on items he is not to chew on, a simple correction is usually enough. Softly swat him on the bottom of his chin and take the forbidden item away from him. This is also a good time to teach your puppy to seek his own chew toys out of the toy box you have provided him. After you have corrected him, lead him over to his box to select a proper "approved" toy. As time goes by you will see your puppy approach the toy box on his own. Be sure to praise him anytime he picks a toy out of the box.

As irritating as it may be to us, chewing is a natural instinct for most puppies. Selecting and carefully monitoring the toys we provide our puppies will help with the problem.

Toy Recommendations: First, look to see what kinds of toys you have given your puppy. A puppy cannot distinguish the difference between old and new. Chances are you have given him old shoes and stuffed animals as puppy toys. He will assume that objects with the same smell (leather, your personal scent) are fair

game. The more items you give your puppy the more difficult it will be for him to realize the difference between proper chew toys and your valuable possessions.

Purchase or use only hard rubber or nyla-bone indestructible chew toys for your puppy. These toys are designed for teething. Many are even beef-scented, making them very attractive as well as safe for your dog. Leather chew toys, such as rawhide, can sometimes be dangerous to many puppies as this is a soft material and can sometimes become lodged in the intestines, causing obstructions. Once your pup has gone through the teething stages, you can give him other toys such as a tennis ball or frisbee.

What Do I Do About Playbiting? Although playbiting may seem innocent, it can lead to a more dangerous form of aggressiveness. It doesn't take long for a puppy to realize that his playbiting scares and intimidates certain people and that this intimidation gives him power.

There are several reasons why young puppies bite. First, a puppy may look upon you as a replacement for his litter mates and playbiting is how he communicates. Second, he may be teething. Although most puppies do not realize how sharp their teeth are and probably mean no real harm by it, you must quickly correct this nipping and do it without destroying his faith and trust in you.

Most of us don't object to our puppy's mouthing our hands softly, but this should only be allowed when initiated by you as a part of playtime and should be limited, as it may be confusing to

your puppy. Grabbing your puppy's muzzle and squeezing it with just enough pressure to cause a little discomfort, lightly shaking it and saying "no, no, no" every time he bites or nips at you, should quickly put an end to unwanted playbiting. However, in extreme cases you may have to apply a collar and leash on your dog and snap the leash when he attempts to snap at you, again keeping in mind not to scream or lose your temper.

Teaching or allowing your puppy to lick more than on occasion is another habit you will most likely want to halt in the beginning. Your friends and family may not appreciate excessive licking, especially later on when your puppy is grown. You have to decide how much licking you will allow before you say enough is enough. Once it starts, licking is a hard habit to break. To correct this, apply the same techniques as those used for playbiting.

Possessiveness: Growling and Biting Over Food and Toys. Growling or biting when someone comes near the puppy's food or toys does not necessarily mean your puppy has turned against you or other people. After all, for thousands of years dogs had to fight for survival, protecting what was theirs instinctively. And, even though your puppy may not have to fight to survive, those instincts are still there. Many puppies learned this reaction from their litter mates who fought to get enough to eat at feeding

ime. That is not to say that this behavior shouldn't be stopped; if you don't, he may think that he can dominate you and his environment in other ways as well. In fact, it could even lead to much more serious behavior, such as severely biting you, a guest or worse mauling a child. You should be able to take the food away from any puppy while they are still eating.

Preventing this behavior is far and away better than trying to correct it later when the puppy is full grown. From the first time you feed your new puppy, take the food away two or three times while he is eating. If he growls or tries to snap at you, put his collar and leash on him and try this exercise again, snapping the leash repeatedly every time he growls or tries to bite at you. This will soon put an end to his possessive /aggressive behavior. This same exercise can be used with object or toy possessiveness.

Note: Snapping the leash does not mean inflicting unnecessary pain on your puppy. It simply means correcting the puppy with a quick snap of the leash and an immediate release of the collar, while simultaneously saying the word "no." You will notice most times we suggest saying "no" while leash correcting. This is to ensure that your dog will obey the command "no" later when he is off leash.

B reaking The Jumping Up Habit: Most dogs learn the habit of jumping while they are puppies. Many times owners encourage their puppies to jump up on them as a part of play. Sometimes they are even praised for this action. By doing this, most puppies learn very early in life that all they have to do to get attention is jump up. The problem is, there will be times when you don't want your puppy to jump up on you or anyone else. If you have taught him that jumping is fun or cute, he will not understand why you sometimes become angry when he later jumps up on you.

It is one thing for a small puppy to jump up and greet someone. It is entirely different for a grown dog to jump up and greet someone, especially a small child.

If you are going to allow your dog to jump up, I strongly recommend you only allow him to do this if you pat your knees with both hands while saying his name and the command, "up". However, if you are going to have a large dog around children or you see that he is beginning to develop a serious jumping habit, put a stop to the jumping action while your puppy is still young. Approach your dog in an excited mood. As he starts to also get excited and jumps up, take your knee (either one or either foot for smaller puppies) and bump your dog with enough impact to knock him off balance, saying the word, "no" at the same time. Repeat this exercise until your puppy makes no attempt to jump up on you or other members of the household or guests. Depending upon how severe his jumping habit is, you will need to set him up for this exercise several times a week for a couple of months. Alternate people during this correction and don't forget to reach down and praise him physically and verbally for his new improved manners.

Calming The Aggressive Puppy. Some puppies are born more dominant than others and are more likely to get out of control at an early age. If you have a puppy that attempts to dominate you or family members, you will want to quickly establish yourself as the person (or persons) in control. If you are already feeling intimidated by your puppy, or if you have a large domineering dog, I would recommend consulting a professional trainer as soon as possible. Things can quickly get out of control. However, if you feel confident in your ability to handle the puppy, begin by attempting the alpha roll exercise.

If you feel the need, use a heavy leather welder's glove. The purpose of the glove is to protect your hand from any scratching or snapping your puppy may do while being held down.

Gently roll your puppy on to his back as shown , holding him down against the floor with just enough pressure to prevent him from turning onto his side or getting up. Within a matter of seconds your puppy will begin to squirm and scratch, trying to escape. The more dominant the puppy, the longer and harder the struggle - some may even snap and growl at you. Hold your puppy in this position until he stops struggling and then continue to hold him in this position for approximately 30 seconds longer. Talk to him in a soothing voice while he is being held down. If he begins to snap at you, say "no" in a very firm, but not loud, voice. Soon he will submit to your authority. Under no circumstances should you lose your temper.

This exercise is designed to show your puppy who is in charge. By restraining the puppy in a rather helpless position, he soon realizes you are in control of his life.

This exercise should not be used on a puppy who is sixteen weeks of age or older. If your puppy is that age and is still trying to dominate you, you will need to begin a program of serious obedience training. With any puppy, obedience training is the key to a successful long term relationship.

Note: Many puppy owners make the mistake of allowing their dog to growl at another dog, acting like they think it's real macho or brave, especially when it is done against a larger dog or a strange person coming to the door. By not correcting this behavior, you are sending the wrong message and encouraging your puppy to act out aggressively.

Excessive Barking: Although barking is a form of communication for dogs, excessive barking is of great annoyance to your family and neighbors. Many suburbs have noise ordinances that include barking dogs, with a fine that can reach as high as $500.00.

Most of us appreciate the fact that our dogs warn us of approaching strangers and want our dogs to bark. To prevent unnecessary barking we must acknowledge our dogs warning by saying O.K.. This is then followed by the word "NO". If your puppy continues to bark, place your hand around his mouth squeezing lightly as you shake his muzzle saying "ENOUGH".

You will find that the more you socialize your puppy around people the easier this problem is to work out.

TOPIC 5-EXERCISING YOUR PUPPY

All puppies need exercise. Most are good self exercisers and usually a small amount of encouragement from you is all they

need. Playing ball or running freely with your puppy on grass is the recommended way to exercise.

Long daily walks on concrete or other hard surfaces are not recommended for large boned puppies such as Shepherds, Rottweilers and Labradors until they are approximately 1 year old and have matured into their adult muscular and skeletal size.

Depending on the development of your puppy's hips, walking or playing on a concrete surface can also cause early arthritis. Once your puppy has reached the age of one year, you can begin to take him for long walks on concrete walkways. Even then, build gradually. Begin with a one block walk and increase each week until you are walking the desired distance. Jogging is OK if the dog's bone structure has developed properly. Check with your veterinarian about your pet's hip development before you jog long distances with him.

If your puppy begins to slow down or drag behind you, it is usually an indication he is finished and needs to be taken home immediately.

Unfortunately, most puppies who have a keen play drive do not know enough to slow down or quit and therefore risk heat stress or heat stroke during the summer season or in warmer climates. Never over-exercise your puppy in extreme temperatures, be they hot or cold.

TOPIC 6-LEASH AND COLLAR TRAINING

If your puppy has a "headstrong" or dominant personality, you may want to begin with a training collar. Although this collar is frequently referred to as a "choke" collar, it should not be used in a choking manner and should never be used to harm a puppy or adult dog. The training collar is intended to provide you some additional leverage. However, if your dog is fairly even-tempered, a leather or nylon collar will probably do just fine. Leashes, too, come in a variety of materials and sizes. The nylon leash comes in different thicknesses and may be a good choice for puppies or smaller breeds of dogs. However, I recommend using a quality leather leash five to six feet in length. Use a 3/8 inch for a toy breed and 1/2 inch for puppies weighing fifteen to thirty pounds.

Training collars should barely slip over the puppy's head and should only be left on while the puppy is being supervised. Puppies with collars on should never be left in a crate or cage as they can become caught on any sharp edges and choke to death.

Getting Accustomed To The Collar and Leash: The first day, leave the collar on as long as possible (most of the day). This should allow your puppy to become accustomed to the feel of a collar around the neck. The second day add the leash. Let him drag it around. Do not try to guide or correct him with the leash; let him step on it and correct himself. If he does this often enough he will not be annoyed with you when you correct him.

27

On the third day, take him for a short walk using both the collar and leash. Begin by walking to places he likes and with which he is comfortable. It should not take him long to become adjusted to his new collar and leash.

Note: Allowing your puppy to pull on the leash, attempting to drag you along as you walk, may cause serious problems as he grows bigger. It is best to correct him now by snapping him back with just enough leverage to teach him not to pull, and by simultaneously saying "no".

TOPIC 7-THIS AND THAT ABOUT YOUR NEW PUPPY

Canine Personalities develop in much the same way as human personalities. Various personality types occur because of the genetics of breeding as well as learned attitudes (environment).

Many dog owners make the mistake of thinking that if they buy a Collie, they will own Lassie. It is the Collie's nature to be a devoted companion, but Lassie's personality was a result of learned behavior from hours of training.

Breed characteristics have been defined over a long period of time and are generalizations of overall temperament. This genetic temperament often stems from the dog's original breeding purpose.

Through proper socialization and training you can help your puppy develop and/or correct many personality faults.

The Security Dog: If your puppy was purchased for security reasons, it is critical he receive sound obedience training before you even consider other training. Additionally, don't be afraid of over socializing your dog. It will not jeopardize his ability to learn to be protective as he matures into adulthood. A dog that has not received obedience training or has not been properly socialized can be very dangerous to its owner as well as others.

Love and Respect: Most dogs innately realize that humans are superior to them, while some consider themselves equal to, or better than, their owners. In either case, taking charge is important. Puppies/dogs become frustrated and confused in an environment lacking in leadership. Through training, your puppy will learn to respect you. While love is a critical element in your

28